THE SACRED TREE

Dedicated to the countless clans, tribes and nation
of indigenous people throughout Mother Earth
whose sacred visions, dreams, prayers, songs,
wisdom, experience and kind guidance form the
foundation and living reality of the *Sacred Tree*.

Produced Collaboratively by:
Judie Bopp, Michael Bopp, Lee Brown and Phil Lane

Illustrations by:
Patricia Lucas

Four Worlds Development Press
Four Worlds Development Project
University of Lethbridge
4401 University Drive
Lethbridge, Alberta, Canada T1K 3M4

Project Coordinator:
Phil Lane

Funding provided by:
National Native Alcohol and Drug Abuse Program
of Health and Welfare Canada

Published in the USA (third edition 1989) by:
Lotus Light Publications
Box 325
Twin Lakes, WI 53181

ISBN 0-941524-58-2
Library of Congress #89-63193
Printed in the United States of America

The Four Worlds Development Project is the result of many people's efforts and wisdom. Some were directly involved, others inspired us through their work in education and alcohol and drug abuse prevention.

Direction for this project was set at a conference held in Lethbridge, Alberta in December, 1982. Participants at the conference were Native elders, spiritual leaders and professionals of various Native communities in North America. Their contributions were framed by their deep commitment to Native people and their own, often hard won, experience. To each of them we offer our deepest respect and appreciation.

Harold Belmont
Mark Belmont
Andy Black Water
Ed Calf Robe
Steve Courchene
Ricki Devlon
Tyrone Eagle Bear
Perry Fontaine
Leonard George
Cindy Ginnish
George Good Striker
Rufus Good Striker
Woodrow Good Striker
Ed Heavy Shields
Peter Heffernan
Lionel Kinunwa

Germaine Kinunwa
Phil Lane, Sr.
John Many Chiefs
Sandy Many Chiefs
Jon Metric
Allan Murray
Wilson Okeymaw
Lee Piper
Doreen Rabit
Chuck Ross
Jerry Saddle Back
Herman Saulis
Frank Sovka
Eric Tootoosis
Mike White
Rose Yellow Feet

Editorial Note:

In English it is impossible to refer to a person without using a pronoun that indicates gender or sex (e.g. he or she, him or her, his or hers). Since there is no special word to refer to a person whose gender is not known, most writers have chosen to use the masculine form in these situations.

This custom of using the masculine form when referring to a person who is not known to be a female, has caused a conspicuous absence of reference to women in English writing.

Thus all of the great ideas and discoveries discussed in English literature are expressed in masculine terms and the reader constantly visualizes males, rather than females, as active participators in the world. Our society's tendency to devalue the role and contributions of women is only augmented by this lack of picturing women in an active, creative role.

The Four Worlds Development Project has chosen to alternate the use of feminine and masculine pronouns whenever the reference is unspecific. This choice of usage is a deliberate one to avoid the awkwardness of the compound form (he/she; him or her) while at the same time acknowledging the harmful consequences of bowing to a convention that persistently forces its audience to visualize the world as dominated by men and operating on ideas expressed in masculine terms.

Table of Contents

"Then I was standing on the highest mountain of them all, and round about beneath me was the whole hoop of the world. And while I stood there I saw more than I can tell and I understood more than I saw; for I was seeing in a sacred manner the shapes of all things in the spirit, and the shape of all shapes as they must live together like one being. And I saw that the sacred hoop of my people was one of many hoops that made one circle, wide as daylight and as starlight, and in the center grew one mighty flowering tree to shelter all the children of one mother and one father. And I saw that it was holy."

Black Elk

(*Black Elk Speaks*, as told through John G. Neihardt, University of Nebraska Press, Lincoln, 1961)

I. THE STORY OF THE SACRED TREE

For all the people of the earth, the Creator has planted a *Sacred Tree* under which they may gather, and there find healing, power, wisdom and security. The roots of this tree spread deep into the body of Mother Earth. Its branches reach upward like hands praying to Father Sky. The fruits of this tree are the good things the Creator has given to the people: teachings that show the path to love, compassion, generosity, patience, wisdom, justice, courage, respect, humility and many other wonderful gifts.

The ancient ones taught us that the life of the Tree is the life of the people. If the people wander far away from the protective shadow of the Tree, if they forget to seek the nourishment of its fruit, or if they should turn against the Tree and attempt to destroy it, great sorrow will fall upon the people. Many will become sick at heart. The people will lose their power. They will cease to dream dreams and see visions. They will begin to quarrel among themselves over worthless trifles. They will become unable to tell the truth and to deal with each other honestly. They will forget how to survive in their own land. Their lives will become filled with anger and gloom. Little by little they will poison themselves and all they touch.

It was foretold that these things would come to pass, but that the Tree would never die. And as long as the Tree lives, the people live. It was also foretold that the day would come when the people would awaken, as if from a long, drugged sleep; that they would begin, timidly at first but then with great urgency, to search again for the *Sacred Tree*.

The knowledge of its whereabouts, and of the fruits that adorn its branches have always been carefully guarded and preserved within the minds and hearts of our wise elders and leaders. These humble, loving and dedicated souls will guide anyone who is honestly and sincerely seeking along the path leading to the protecting shadow of the *Sacred Tree*.

II. IMPORTANT CONCEPTS

Symbols

Symbols express and represent meaning. Meaning
helps provide purpose and
understanding in the lives of
human beings. Indeed to live
without symbols is to experience existence far short of its
full meaning. Ways of express-
ing and representing meaning
include the symbol systems of
mathematics, spoken and writ-
ten language and the arts.

The Medicine Wheel

This is an ancient symbol used by almost all the Native people of North and South America. There are many different ways that this basic concept is expressed: the four grandfathers, the four winds, the four cardinal directions, and many other relationships that can be expressed in sets of four. Just like a mirror can be used to see things not normally visible (e.g. behind us or around a corner), the medicine wheel can be used to help us see or understand things we can't quite see or understand because they are ideas and not physical objects.

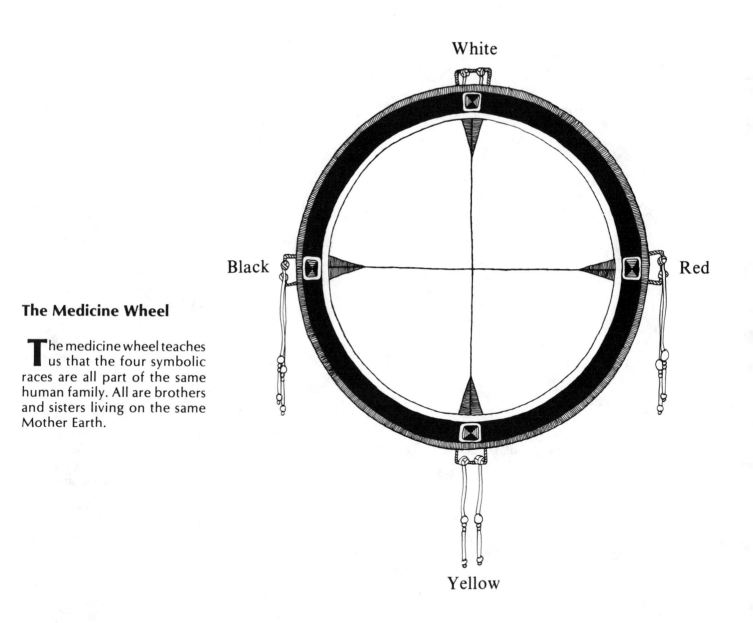

White

Black

Red

Yellow

The Medicine Wheel

The medicine wheel teaches us that the four symbolic races are all part of the same human family. All are brothers and sisters living on the same Mother Earth.

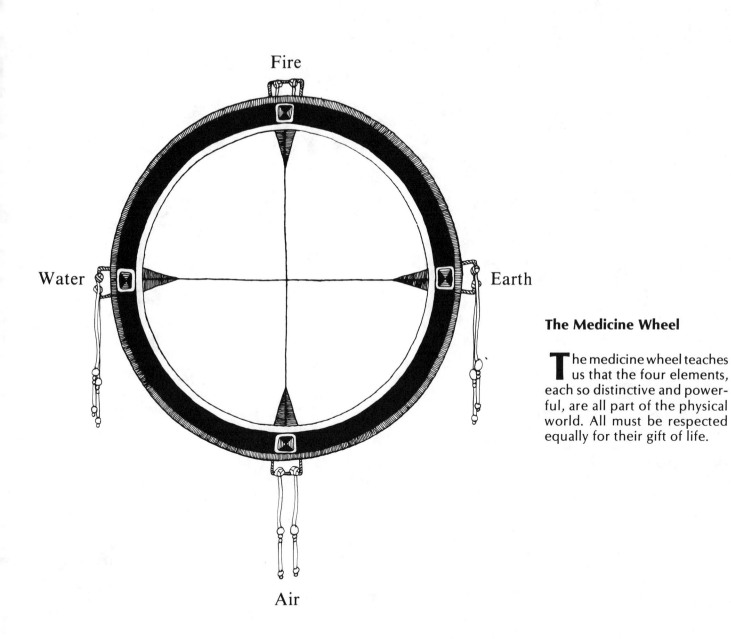

Fire

Water

Earth

Air

The Medicine Wheel

The medicine wheel teaches us that the four elements, each so distinctive and powerful, are all part of the physical world. All must be respected equally for their gift of life.

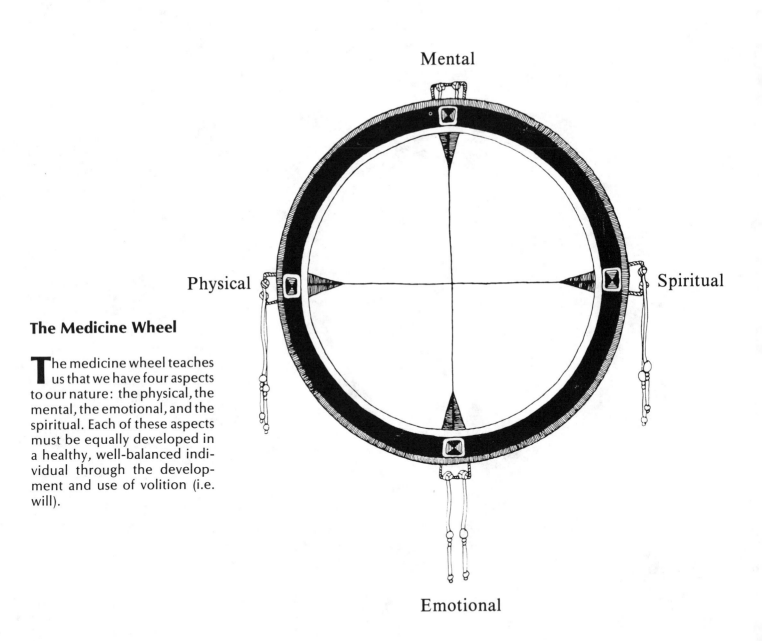

Mental

Physical

Spiritual

Emotional

The Medicine Wheel

The medicine wheel teaches us that we have four aspects to our nature: the physical, the mental, the emotional, and the spiritual. Each of these aspects must be equally developed in a healthy, well-balanced individual through the development and use of volition (i.e. will).

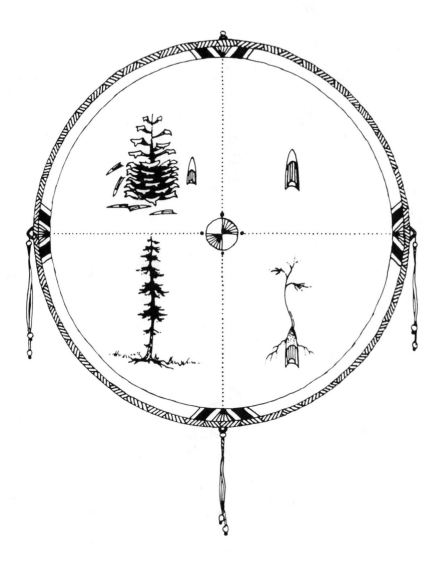

Potential

Potentially the seed has a mighty tree within it. The four aspects of our nature (the physical, the mental, the emotional and the spiritual) are like seeds. They have the potential to grow into powerful gifts.

Volition

We can use our volition (i.e. our will) to help us develop the four aspects of our nature. Volition is the force that helps us make decisions and then act to carry out those decisions. We can learn to exercise our volition by carring out each of its five steps:

1. attention (concentration)
2. goal setting
3. initiating the action
4. perseverance
5. completing the action

Since volition is a primary force in developing all of our human potentialities, it is placed at the center of the medicine wheel.

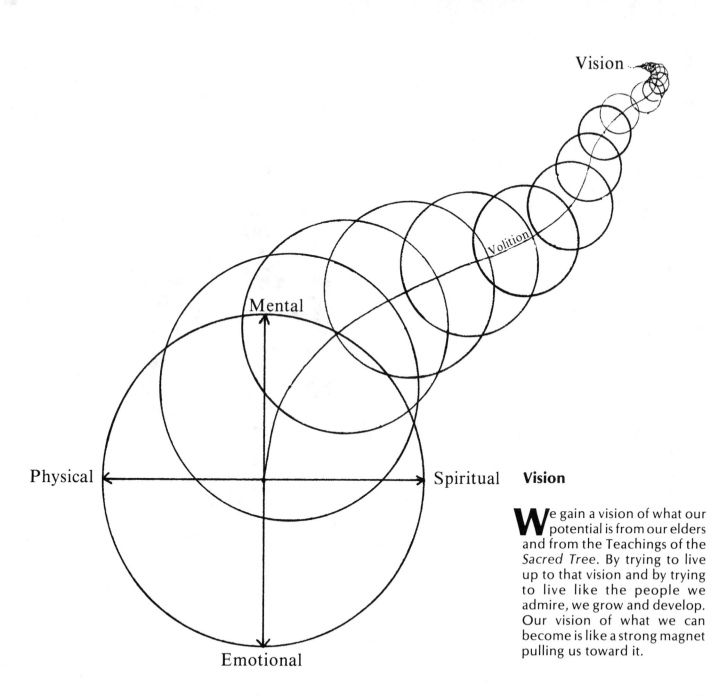

Vision

Volition

Mental

Physical

Spiritual

Emotional

Vision

We gain a vision of what our potential is from our elders and from the Teachings of the *Sacred Tree*. By trying to live up to that vision and by trying to live like the people we admire, we grow and develop. Our vision of what we can become is like a strong magnet pulling us toward it.

Growth and Change

All human beings have the capacity to grow and change. The four aspects of our nature (the physical, the mental, the emotional, and the spiritual) can be developed when we have a vision of what is possible and when we use our volition to change our actions and our attitudes so that they will be closer to our vision of a happy, healthy human being.

Identity

A person's identity consists of:

Body awareness: how you experience your physical presence

Self-concept: what you think about yourself and your potential

Self-esteem: how you feel about yourself and your ability to grow and change

Self-determination: your ability to use your volition (will) to actualize your physical, mental, emotional and spiritual potentialities

Values

Values are the way human beings pattern and use their energy. If there is not a balance between our values concerning ourselves and our values concerning others, we cannot continue to develop our true potential as human beings. Indeed, if there is an imbalance, individuals, and whole communities suffer and even die.

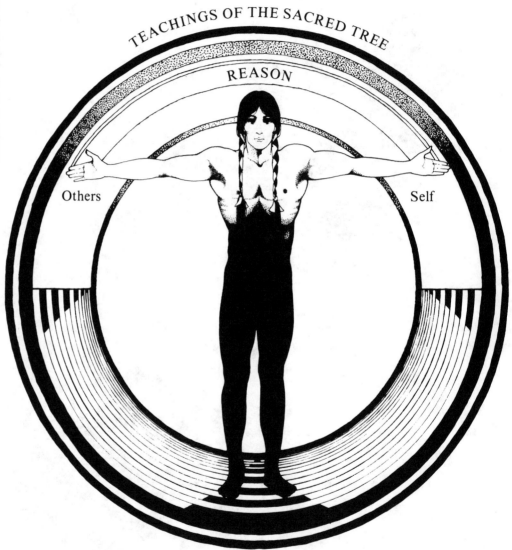

III. THE SYMBOLIC TEACHINGS OF THE SACRED TREE

Introduction

Symbols such as the *Sacred Tree* express and represent meaning. Meaning helps to provide purpose and understanding in the lives of human beings. Symbols can be found on the walls of the first caves of human existence and have guided us to the far reaches of space in our attempts to understand life's meaning. Through the experience of human consciousness, symbols are eternally giving birth to new understandings of the essence of life as it emerges, ever elusive, out of the unknown mist of creation. Symbols thus create an ever increasing awareness of the ongoing flow of life and give meaning to each sunrise and more meaning to each sunset.

Meaning is important for the health, well-being and wholeness of individuals and communities. The presence of symbols in a community, as well as the living out of a belief in these symbols, is a measurement of the health and energies present in the community. Indeed, to live without symbols is to experience existence far short of our unlimited capacity as human beings. Thus every rebirth of the life and purpose of a people is accompanied by the revitalization of that people's symbols.

The Symbol of the Sacred Tree

The *Sacred Tree* as a symbol of life-giving meaning is of vital importance to the indigenous peoples of the earth. For countless generations it has provided meaning and inspiration for many tribes and nations. The *Sacred Tree* is a symbol around which lives, religions, beliefs and nations have been organized. It is a symbol of profound depth, capable of providing enough meaning for a lifetime of reflection.

The *Sacred Tree* represents life, cycles of time, the earth, and the universe. The meanings of the *Sacred Tree* reflect the teachings of the medicine wheel. The center of this medicine wheel is the symbolic center of creation and of the tribe. This meaning is reflected in a song which is sung on behalf of the *Sacred Tree* chosen for the sun dance.

> *I am standing*
> *In a sacred way*
> *At the earth's center*
> *Beheld by the people,*
> *Seeing the tribe*
> *Gathered around me.   (Lamedeer)*

(*Seeker of Visions*, by John Fire Lamedeer and Richard Eros, Simon and Schuster, New York, 1972, p. 205.)

The Four Great Meanings of the Sacred Tree

The meanings of the *Sacred Tree* may be organized into four major categories. These categories may be easily viewed as movements in the cycle of human development from our birth toward our unity with the wholeness of creation. The four great meanings of the *Sacred Tree* are:

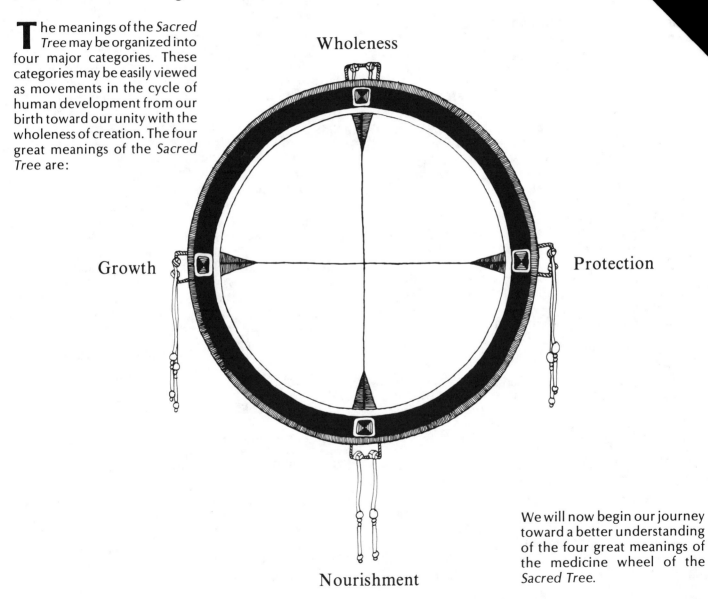

Wholeness

Growth

Protection

Nourishment

We will now begin our journey toward a better understanding of the four great meanings of the medicine wheel of the *Sacred Tree*.

21

he Sacred Tree

s a symbol of protection. The
provides protection from the
rce of material for homes and
ich provide physical and spirit-
tree provides firewood which
g... p......... the cold. The bark of the *Sacred Tree* represents protection from the outside world. The *Sacred Tree* provides the material from which kayaks and canoes are made. The greatest protection of the *Sacred Tree* is to provide a gathering place and central pole of unity for the people.

Symbolically, the *Sacred Tree* represents a gathering place for the many different tribes and peoples of the world. The *Sacred Tree* provides a place of protection in the world, a place of peace, contemplation, and centering. Like our mother's womb which provided nourishment and protection during the earliest days of our life, the *Sacred Tree* may be thought of as a womb of protection which gives birth to our values and potentialities as unique human beings.

The process of developing our uniqueness through the teachings of the *Sacred Tree* gives rise to a vision, not of what we are, but of what we can become. That vision becomes the path toward our wholeness. Thus we see in the symbolic protection of the *Sacred Tree* the beginning of our wholeness and the emergence of the seed of our potential.

The Nourishment of the Sacred Tree

The second symbolic meaning of the *Sacred Tree* is the nourishment we need to live and grow. This nourishment is symbolically represented by the fruit of the tree. On one level the fruit of the *Sacred Tree* represents the nourishment a mother gives to her children and all the care children should receive as they are growing up.

A deeper meaning of the fruit is the nurturing human beings receive through interactions with the human, physical and spiritual environments. These environments are often symbolically represented by the mother. Hence, interaction with the tree and eating the fruit of the tree symbolically represent our interaction with all the aspects of life that nourish and sustain our growth and development.

The leaves of the *Sacred Tree* represent people. Eventually the leaves of the tree fall to earth and provide nourishment for the continued health, growth and future flowering of the *Sacred Tree*. Symbolically, this represents the passing of the generations and the spiritual teachings they leave behind for the health and growth of those that come after them. This symbolic meaning of the tree emphasizes the necessity of using the accumulated wisdom of the past to nourish the present and to plan for the future. This wisdom arises from the hard-won experience of countless generations and is taught through the songs, dances, stories, prayers and ceremonies of the people. Thus this wisdom provides nourishment for the development of each generation's potentiality.

Another symbolic teaching of the leaf is sacrifice. The leaves sacrifice themselves for the future of the *Sacred Tree*. This is symbolic of the ceremonial sacrifices made on behalf of the life of the tribe and the health of the community. This teaching reflects the belief that a human being's growth during his life is equal to his service and sacrifice for others. Therefore, giving and sacrifice not only provide a positive service for the community, but also create further growth in the individual during his existence in this creation.

The Growth of the Sacred Tree

The third symbolic meaning of the *Sacred Tree* is growth. The *Sacred Tree* symbolizes the importance of pursuing life experiences which provide positive growth and development. The *Sacred Tree* grows from its central core outward and upward. This inner growth of the tree symbolizes the need all human beings have for an inner life. Human beings grow in the qualities of the four directions, physically, mentally, emotionally and spiritually, as a result of inner reflection and change. Indeed, changes in a human being often occur internally and are then manifested in the personality of the individual. These changes are often hidden from view while they are occurring just as the inner growth of the *Sacred Tree* is hidden. However, we can see the result of this inner growth in the exterior of the tree. Thus, our outer life can be understood as a reflection of the development of our inner being. By deepening and developing the qualities of the four directions within ourselves, we grow to reflect these spiritual qualities in our daily lives. This is one of the primary spiritual teachings of the medicine wheel represented symbolically in the *Sacred Tree*.

The roots and limbs of the *Sacred Tree* grow toward the four directions. This also represents growth in the spiritual qualities and teachings of the medicine wheel. The growth of these roots and limbs can also be seen as a representation of these qualities reflected in our life's work.

The *Sacred Tree* teaches us the importance of having great respect for our inner spiritual growth as human beings. The inner growth of the *Sacred Tree* sends forth its roots and limbs, as if in prayer, to the four directions. Our own inner growth is manifested in our daily life and affects our relationship to the four directions. Symbolically this represents the four dimensions of learning and the development of the four aspects of human nature represented on the medicine wheel.

In another sense the growth of the tree represents cycles of time and of life. The changes in the *Sacred Tree* during the changing seasons of the year represent the many changes in our life as we grow and develop in our relationship to creation, a life-long process of becoming our own true self. This is an eternal process that reaches beyond life itself. The *Sacred Tree* is rooted in Mother Earth but reaches upward toward a limitless universe. This symbolic growth developed through struggle and self-determination is ever rewarded by the development of many new and wonderful gifts for ourselves and our communities.

The Wholeness of the Sacred Tree

The fourth meaning of the *Sacred Tree* is wholeness. Symbolically the wholeness of the *Sacred Tree* is the unity and centering of the qualities of the four directions in the human being. This meaning is reflected in the words of Lamedeer about the *Sacred Tree* chosen for the sun dance pole:

> *When the tree finally arrived in the camp circle a great shout of joy rose from all the people . . . The top of the pole was decorated with strips of coloured cloth, one each for the four corners of the earth. (Lamedeer)*

The *Sacred Tree* represents the Great Spirit as the center pole of creation, a center for balancing and understanding ourselves as human beings. The teachings of the *Sacred Tree* provide a foundation for organizing our values and a safe path for developing and protecting the wholeness of our being. This balance and understanding is based on the unity of the elements of creation brought to life in the tree. This unity is achieved in ourselves by understanding and balancing the opposite yet related qualities of life and in our process of growth as human beings. From one point of view the unseen roots in Mother Earth represent the invisible aspects of our being and the part of the *Sacred Tree* above ground represents those aspects that are visible. When we understand and balance these parts of our self, the tree of our being will grow rich with abundant fruit that contains the seeds of yet further growth, development and wholeness.

In truth, we begin our lives with wholeness, but we have experiences as individuals in our families, tribes, and from society that sometimes shatter and fragment this wholeness. If we have been hurt, this wholeness can be restored and its development enhanced through the natural healing processes and spiritual lessons contained within the teachings of the *Sacred Tree*.

Conclusion

We began by stating that the *Sacred Tree* provides enough meaning for a lifetime of reflection. Here we have only briefly touched the surface of the ocean of its symbolic meanings. Still, we can begin to see the depths of its meanings as if looking into the surface waters of a deep pool. To reflect and act upon the teachings of the *Sacred Tree* is to renew the life of humanity. To use this symbol is to move toward the wholeness promised in the prophecies of this time; a time of purification and renewal of all life in creation; a time of gathering together through the protection, nourishment, growth and wholeness of the *Sacred Tree*.

IV. FIRST PRINCIPLES

What follows is a summary of some of the important teachings of the *Sacred Tree*. Each one of them is a gate opening onto a path. It is for the traveler to step through the gate and begin the journey.

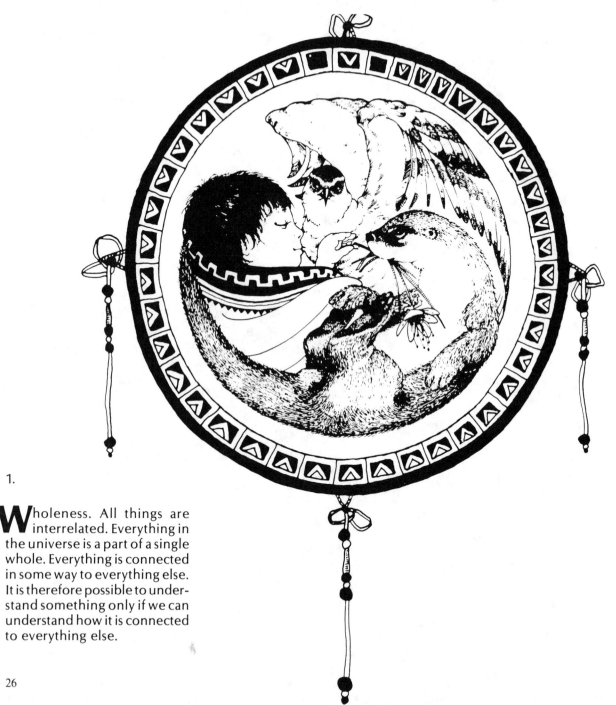

1.

Wholeness. All things are interrelated. Everything in the universe is a part of a single whole. Everything is connected in some way to everything else. It is therefore possible to understand something only if we can understand how it is connected to everything else.

26

3.

Changes occur in cycles or patterns. They are not random or accidental. Sometimes it is difficult to see how a particular change is connected to everything else. This usually means that our standpoint (the situation from which we are viewing the change) is limiting our ability to see clearly.

2.

Change. All of creation is in a state of constant change. Nothing stays the same except the presence of cycle upon cycle of change. One season falls upon the other. Human beings are born, live their lives, die and enter the spirit world. All things change. There are two kinds of change. The coming together of things (development) and the coming apart of things (disintegration). Both of these kinds of change are necessary and are always connected to each other.

4.

The seen and the unseen. The physical world is real. The spiritual world is real. These two are aspects of one reality. Yet, there are separate laws which govern each of them. Violation of spiritual laws can affect the physical world. Violation of physical laws can affect the spiritual world. A balanced life is one that honors the laws of both of these dimensions of reality.

5.

Human beings are spiritual
as well as physical.

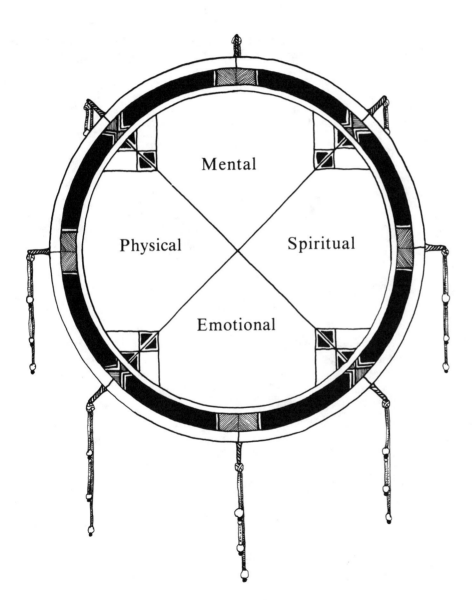

Mental

Physical   Spiritual

Emotional

6.

Human beings can always acquire new gifts, but they must struggle to do so. The timid may become courageous, the weak may become bold and strong, the insensitive may learn to care for the feelings of others and the materialistic person can acquire the capacity to look within and to listen to her inner voice. The process human beings use to develop new qualities may be called "true learning".

7.

There are four dimensions of "true learning". These four aspects of every person's nature are reflected in the four cardinal points of the medicine wheel. These four aspects of our being are developed through the use of our volition. It cannot be said that a person has totally learned in a whole and balanced manner unless all four dimensions of her being have been involved in the process.

8.

The spiritual dimension of human development may be understood in terms of four related capacities.

First, the capacity to have and to respond to realities that exist in a non-material way such as dreams, visions, ideals, spiritual teachings, goals and theories.

Second, the capacity to accept those realities as a reflection (in the form of symbolic representation) of unknown or unrealized potential to do or be something more or different than we are now.

Third, the capacity to express these nonmaterial realities using symbols such as speech, art or mathematics.

Fourth, the capacity to use this symbolic expression to guide future action - action directed toward making what was only seen as a possibility into a living reality.

9.

Human beings must be active participants in the unfolding of their own potentialities.

10.

The doorway through which all must pass if they wish to become more or different than they are now is the doorway of the will (volition). A person must *decide* to take the journey. The path has infinite patience. It will always be there for those who decide to travel it.

11.

Anyone who sets out (i.e. makes a commitment and then acts on that commitment) on a journey of self-development will be aided. There will be guides and teachers who will appear, and spiritual protectors to watch over the traveler. No test will be given that the traveler does not already have the strength to meet.

12.

The only source of failure on a journey will be the traveler's own failure to follow the teachings of the *Sacred Tree*.

V. THE GIFTS OF THE FOUR DIRECTIONS

Introduction

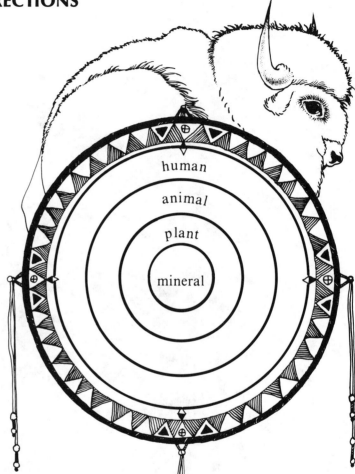

The Medicine Wheel

The medicine wheel is an ancient and powerful symbol of the Universe. It is a silent teacher of the realities of things. It shows the many different ways in which all things are interconnected. Beyond that, it shows not only things that are, but also things that could be.

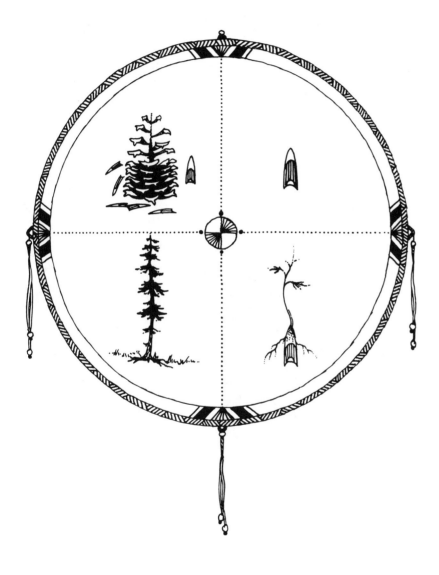

When the medicine wheel is used as a mirror by sincere human beings, it shows that within them are hidden many wonderful gifts that have not yet been developed. For the medicine wheel can show us not only as we are now, but also as we could be if we were to develop the potential gifts the Creator has deposited within us.

Many of these hidden potentialities might never be developed if we did not somehow discover and nuture them, for as the great spiritual teachers have taught, all the gifts a person potentially possesses are like the fruits hidden within the tree.

It cannot be said that the fruit which has not yet appeared on the tree is a reality, and yet again it cannot be said that the fruit has no reality, because it does indeed exist potentially. It is a wonderful spiritual power given to human beings by the Creator to be able to see potential as another dimension of reality and then to decide and act to realize the potential.

The tree could be cut into a thousand pieces and no new fruit will be found, yet when the conditions are right for its growth (warm sunshine, rain, nourishing soil) the tree will develop the fruit in all of its luscious beauty.

Human beings create many of the necessary conditions for the development of their own potential. They do this through the operation of their will. They decide to do so.

Unless a person decides and acts to provide the necessary conditions for the development of hidden qualities (for example, gifts such as courage, willpower, clear thinking, or an appreciation of beauty), these gifts remain like the fruit hidden within the tree.

The medicine wheel can be used as a model of what human beings could become if they decided and acted to develop their full potential. Each person who looks deeply into the medicine wheel will see things in a slightly different way. This is because the Creator has made each of us to be a unique human being, and given to each of us a special combination of gifts to be used to further develop ourselves and to serve others.

No two people will see exactly the same things when they look deeply into the mirror of the medicine wheel.

Yet everyone who looks deeply will see the tree of their unique lives with its roots buried deep in the soil of universal truths.

Because many tribes and peoples have used the medicine wheel to look at themselves, there are many different ways of explaining those universal truths that human beings share in common.

In our presentation of the medicine wheel on the following pages we have assigned certain qualities (or gifts) to each direction.

We have also chosen certain animals or other aspects of nature to represent qualities or gifts, and lessons.

Even though some tribes will assign different qualities to each of the points on the circle or to different animals than we have, the teachings telling which qualities make up the total picture of a complete human being are nevertheless universal. All representations teach that human beings have

1. physical
2. mental
3. emotional
4. spiritual
5. volitional (will)

aspects to their being. All representations show that the various gifts of the *Sacred Tree* balance one another. Our way of showing this is one way of showing something that is really universal, and as such can be shown in many ways.

Often people use animals to symbolize certain qualities. For example, some have used eagles to symbolize courage, others have used a she-bear or the wolverine to symbolize the same thing. We could say that the wolverine is a "teacher" of courage. By that we mean that when we consider the qualities possessed by our brother the wolverine, we can learn something about human courage. Many cultures throughout Mother Earth use similar symbolic teachers in their stories and lessons.

The reason various aspects of nature are used as symbols is because many of the human qualities reflected in the medicine wheel are difficult to understand without a living example. By choosing examples from the world around them, people are able to look deeply into the nature of the gift they seek to acquire. As each person uses the wheel, they will discover symbols (some animal, some not) that speak deeply and personally to them. It is important that you feel free to use your own symbols as you discover them.

Let us now take a journey together around the medicine wheel. What you will see, if you look deeply within your own being using the medicine wheel as a mirror, is an image of your strengths and weaknesses, and a vision of what you could become if you were to commit your life to the (symbolic) journey of the medicine wheel, which is really the journey of authentic human development.

We will travel around the wheel as the sun travels around the earth, from the east to the west.

We will allow each of the directions to represent certain parts of a fully developing person. We cannot say fully *developed* as if it were all over, because human potential is infinite. Human *developing* never stops.

As you consider the gifts of each of the four directions, you may feel yourself attracted more to some than to others. This may be because of the particular and unique set of gifts the Creator has given especially to you to fulfill your own unique destiny. It may also be because our society emphasizes certain capacities as being somehow better or more desirable than others.

For example, men in many societies are taught that they should be tough, courageous, tenacious and, if need be, hard.

Humility, gentleness, courtesy and a loving heart are considered to be "feminine" qualities and are even laughed at in some groups when these qualities are displayed by a man.

Yet the medicine wheel teaches us that courage must be balanced by wisdom, toughness by gentleness of heart, or perseverance and tenacity by flexibility. A person who does not achieve these balances in her life will not be able to develop her full potential as a human being. This is one of the great lessons of the medicine wheel.

As we journey around the wheel, reflect on your own qualities and gifts. Certainly, the fundamental value of this tool (the medicine wheel) is a way of measuring our own progress and development, and a means for assessing what we must work on next in our journey through life.

One final warning is needed. It is dangerous to categorize yourself as a "northern person" or an "eastern person". In order to use the wheel correctly, you must visualize yourself in the center of the wheel, connected equally to all points by the power of your will.

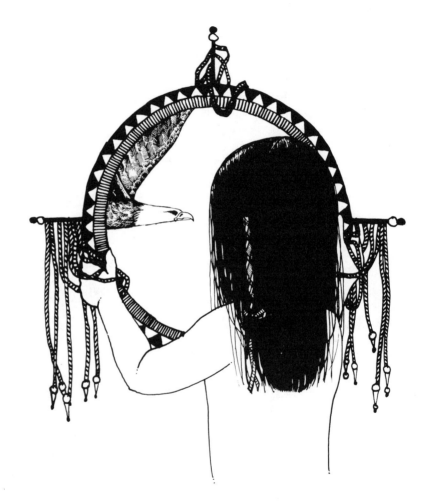

Our journey around the wheel is a symbolic one. What we are really doing is using the patterns found in nature, such as the turning of the seasons, to understand our own selves. We can do this because the universe, in all of its splendor and complexity, is reflected within our own beings.

The medicine wheel is a symbolic tool that helps us to see that interconnectedness of our being with the rest of creation.

A. The Gifts of the East

The East is the direction from which the new day comes into the world. It is the direction of renewal. It is the place of innocence, guilelessness, spontaneity, joy and the capacity to believe in the unseen.

When we travel to the East we will be tested with lessons that will teach us many things. There we will learn of warmth of spirit, purity, trust, hope, and the uncritical acceptance of others. We will learn to love as a child loves; a love that does not question others and does not know itself. Here courage is born and truthfulness begins.

The East is the place of all beginnings. The human being must return many times to the East in the course of a life's journey. Each time, there will be new things to learn on a new level of understanding.

The capacity to watch over and guard the well-being of others is an important gift, and one that is learned with great difficulty. For it is one thing to see the situation others are in, but it is quite another to care enough about them to want to help, and yet another to know what to do.

In the East of the medicine wheel, a good leader learns to see things as they are connected to all other things, to be self-reliant, to have hope for the people and to trust in his vision. But until the journey is made to the South of the wheel (the place of the heart), there to learn of sacrifice, of sensitivity to others' feelings, of love that expects nothing in return; and until

Not only is the East the direction of birth and rebirth, it is also the direction of illumination. It is the direction from which light comes into the world. Hence it is the direction of guidance and leadership. Here the gifts of beautiful and clear speech that help others to understand is acquired. Also, the ability to see clearly through complex situations and over a long time is learned. Like the eagle, a leader of the people must often travel alone. The eagle flies high above the world. It watches the movements of all the creatures and knows the hiding place of even the tiniest of them.

the journey is made to the West to learn of one's unique purpose, to learn how to correctly use power, to learn what the Creator would ask of him as a leader, one cannot truly lead the people. And until one journeys to the North, to learn how to serve and guide the people with wisdom, one cannot guide others. It will not be until we journey from the East to the far North of the medicine wheel, to the place of wisdom, that we will realize that within every one of us is hidden the potential to guide others on some part of the journey of the four directions.

Learning to Be in the Here and Now

It is in the East of the medicine wheel that all journeys begin. When a path is new, it totally occupies our attention. Our sights are focused on the next few steps. One of the most important gifts to be acquired in the East is the capacity to focus our attention on the events of the present moment. As young children (the East is also the direction of childhood), we knew instinctively how to do this. When as children we watched a beautiful butterfly or examined any interesting new aspect of the world, we were completely absorbed by what we were doing. We were able to submerge our total awareness into that butterfly, that patch of ground, or that toy. The animal that many have used to symbolize this capacity is the mouse. Our little mouse sister does what she does with all of her tiny being.

Many people cannot do this. They are always looking to the future, or to the past, or inside or outside, or far away, but seldom to the activity of the present moment. It is this capacity of being fully in the present moment that enables a person to accomplish physical tasks that require the alertness of all the senses and the complete giving of ourselves to what we are doing. Examples might include acquiring excellence in hunting, in craftsmanship such as fine beadwork, sewing or woodwork, in the healing arts, in competitive sports or in the playing of a musical instrument. All of these require a merging of the person's total being with the activity at hand. This is the special gift of our little

mouse sister. Learning to do this is the first stage in the development of volition (the power of the human will).

But like the mouse who is caught unaware by the owl because she is so absorbed in gathering seeds that she becomes oblivious to her own danger, a person who has learned this quality in the East must also learn to listen to inner warning signs that rumble like thunder or flash like lightning within us (a lesson of the West), and must have the foresightedness (a lesson of the North) to look at the overall picture (another lesson of the East) in order to ensure his own happiness and well-being.

A person who is too proud or insensitive to listen to others (a gift of the South) or who has never stood in the West of the medicine wheel and looked over to the East to see how vulnerable our little mouse sister really is; such a person may well be too filled with a false sense of his own greatness to be of assistance to the people.

It is no accident that (from one symbolic view) one of the humblest creatures (the mouse) and one of nobility (the eagle) are the twin teachers of the East. For greatness of spirit and humility are opposite sides of the same reality. The essence of true leadership is service to the people.

Indeed the essence of what it is to be a human being is to be found in service to others. This is the greatest of all the lessons of the medicine wheel. In a lifetime, most people must journey many times to the East to relearn this one lesson.

It would take more than one thousand lifetimes to tell of all of the gifts of the East, or any of the direction points on the medicine wheel. The horse that carries the traveler on the journey of search for the gifts of the four directions is named Patience. Without him the traveler could not continue the journey. Let us now continue our symbolic journey around the medicine wheel.

B.   The Gifts of the South

The South is the direction of the sun at its highest point. It is the place of summer, of fullness, of youth, of physical strength and vigor. It is also the time that people work to prepare for the fall and winter months. Hence, symbolically, it is a time of preparing for the future, of getting ready for days ahead.

The South is also the place of the heart, of generosity, of sensitivity to the feelings of others, of loyalty, of noble passions and of love.

But the love learned in the South is not the unconditional love for all of creation that a pure hearted child feels. Nor is it the detached love for the people that our brother the eagle, in his lonely flight above the world, must learn by journeying to the West.

The love learned in the South is the love of one person for another. How we long to be with the one we love. And how easy it is for this longing to change into a desire to possess and control that person - to have her for ourselves. We can remember this lesson by the symbol of the beautiful rose bush, fragrant, delicate and so inviting to the senses and to the hand. And yet, hidden beneath her soft green leaves are piercing thorns that would tear the flesh of anyone who would seize her beauty and try to own if for herself.

The South direction of the medicine wheel is also the great place of testing for the physical body. There we must learn to discipline our bodies as one would train and discipline a wonderful horse, so that it responds to our every command but never attempts to direct our journey.

Many people behave as if they were controlled by their bodies. They cannot separate what their bodies want (certain food or drink, sexual satisfaction, sleep, etc.) from what is true and good. To exercise this kind of discipline requires determination (an aspect of volition, i.e. the will) to fulfill our purposes and achieve our goals. The ability to choose goals and to decide to pursue them is the second stage in the development of the human will.

The senses such as sight, hearing, touch and taste are all gifts of the body that can be trained and developed to serve the whole person.

In the South the traveler also acquires the gifts of music, gracefulness of movement, appreciation of the arts and the powers of discrimination in sight, hearing and taste. One symbol that can be used to represent physical excellence and sensory acuteness is the cougar.

But the cougar is only one of the symbolic teachers of the South. The focused concentration learned in the East from our little mouse sister becomes, in the South, a passionate involvement with the world. In the South the traveler learns the idealism that makes all great causes possible. Idealism is a response of the heart to the beauty or ugliness in the world around us. It is not necessarily rooted in deep spiritual insight (a lesson to be learned in the North direction of the medicine wheel). It is essentially an emotional attraction to what is good or an emotional repulsion by what is evil or harmful.

The development of emotional capacities for love, loyalty, generosity, compassion and kindness on the one hand, and our capacity to be angry at injustice and repulsed by senseless violence, are important lessons to be learned in the South.

On the other hand, to hold in feelings of hurt or anger without being able to release them can be extremely damaging to our physical, emotional, mental and spiritual well-being. There are times when tears of grief run down from Father Sky to Mother Earth so that all of creation might learn to weep. For until feelings of anger, resentment and hurt that the people have taken inside of them can be released and understood, these feelings will continue to block the intelligence and chill the capacities for genuine love and warmth of many human beings.

Our feelings (such as anger, fear or love) do not "happen" to us like a rock dropped on our heads. The popular phrase "falling in love" shows that many people believe that love happens to them. Yet wise teachers and elders know that feelings can be realized and controlled by an act of our will. Indeed, feelings can be refined, evaluated and developed.

Just as the body can be trained and developed through the exercise of the will, so too can our feelings be disciplined. For example, people who fly into uncontrollable anger because they have been denied something they wanted, have not learned to discipline the powers of emotion. People who are so overcome with excitement or fear in an emergency that they are unable to act to help themselves or others, have likewise not learned to discipline their feelings.

The most difficult and valuable gift to be sought in the South of the medicine wheel is the capacity to express feelings openly and freely in ways that do not hurt other beings.

The practical value of this is that we will then have the ability to set aside our feelings of anger, hurt, or grief in order to counsel or in other ways assist other people. We will also be able to appropriately release our own feelings of hurt that prevent us from being a clear-thinking and effective human being.

A symbol of this vital lesson is the red willow tree, the other great teacher of the South. The red willow is both the strongest and the most flexible in the forest. It can survive flood, fire, severe winter, and droughts. Always it yields to forces that would destroy the other trees, but always it springs back. The lesson of our sister the willow may always be remembered by the beautiful music of the whistles and flutes that we make from her branches.

Let us now continue our symbolic journey around the medicine wheel, for there is yet much to be learned.

C. The Gifts of the West

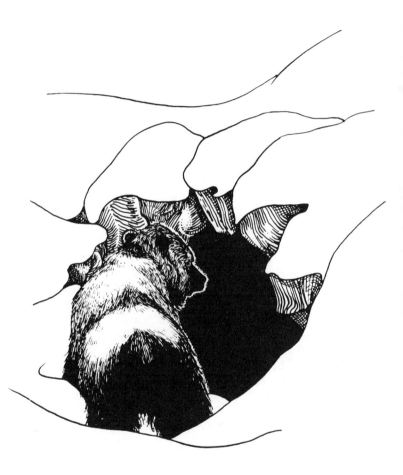

The West is the direction from which darkness comes. It is the direction of the unknown, of going within, of dreams, of prayer and of meditation. The West is the place of testing, where the will is stretched to its outer limits so that the gift of perseverance may be won.

For the nearer one draws toward a goal the more difficult the journey becomes. The capacity to stick to a challenge even though it is very hard and even painful is an important lesson to be learned in the West. Indeed, it is the third great lesson in the development of our will.

Because thunder and lightning often come from there, the West is also the direction (symbolically) of power. In many traditions the West is where the Thunder Beings live. These are the bringers of power. Power to heal. Power to protect and defend. Power to see and to know. Here the traveler must learn to manage power in ways that are in harmony with the great universal teachings of the *Sacred Tree*.

Two teachers of the West (symbolically) are the black bear and the turtle. A person who has traveled to the West and received the gifts that await her there will, like the black bear, possess great strengths. But the source of that strength will come from deep within the person. Like the bear who retires to a dark, private place in the face of winter's coldness, a person who has learned the lessons of the West balances the passionate loyalty of the South with deep spiritual insight. This insight is gained by shutting out the clamor of the world, and by going alone to pray and be tested.

One of the guides on this inner journey can be pictured (symbolically) as the turtle, who not only teaches to go within, but also grants the gift of perseverance to those who learn his ways.

By journeying to the center of one's being, it is possible for a person to experience directly the connection between the human spirit and the rest of the universe, and between the human spirit and the Creator. This experience is the gift of prayer.

To enter the place of learning and testing deep within us requires a great daily effort. Each morning upon rising, and each night before sleeping, the elders have taught us that we must meet our Creator alone. One way to do this is to set aside a room in our house, or a part of a room, or some other special place, and to use that place every day for prayer, meditation and deep personal reflection.

Sacred Objects

Many people collect objects on their journey that have special significance to them. For some it may be a certain book or photograph. For others, it may be things from nature such as a feather, a small stone, or some special herb. These things usually symbolize, to their holder, aspects of that person's spiritual journey through life. Contact with these special objects can have the effect (for those who understand their use) of raising the person's awareness about the deep spiritual significance of the ordinary things of everyday life.

When people understand that it is not the objects themselves that are the source of power, but rather the deep meanings these objects have to the person who uses them, then the use of sacred objects can greatly assist a person to focus himself for prayer and meditation.

No Time for Inner Life

If people find no room in their lives to pray or meditate, to reflect deeply on why they have been created and what they must do with their lives, and to listen with all of their being to the guidance of the universe, then those peole are like birds who have not yet learned to fly. All the parts of the bird are present, but something is still missing. To be a whole person is to be alive in a physical, emotional, mental and spiritual way.

Signs of Spiritual Emptiness

A sign that much work is needed in the area of personal spiritual growth is when a person dislikes being alone, and especially dislikes being alone in silence. Many people use television or recorded music to fill the silence so that they do not have to experience themselves as they really are.

To face ourselves alone in silence, and to love ourselves because the Creator has made us beautiful are things that every developing human being needs to learn. From this position of strength, no one can put us down, and no one can lead us to do or to be anything else but what we know we must do or be.

Another sign that warns the traveler that his heart is empty of the gifts of the West is when a person does not feel respect for the elders, or for the spiritual activities and struggles of other people. To laugh and ridicule spiritual things is to say: I feel an emptiness within me that I must hide by my criticism of others or my pretended laughter.

The Greatest Lesson of the West

The greatest lesson to be learned from the (symbolic) teachers of the West is to accept ourselves as we really are; both spiritual and physical beings, and to never again cut ourselves off from the spiritual part of our nature.

The West is the place of sacrifice. When we stand in the West we learn that nothing may be taken from the universe unless something is given. For each of the great gifts of the medicine wheel there is a price. And yet we will learn that the mystery of sacrifice is that there is no sacrifice.

From the West we can look over to the East, to the place of innocence and first beginnings and there we can see ourselves standing naked to the universe, vulnerable and small before the stars. It is then that we receive the gift of humility.

And we can look over to the South, and there we can see ourselves struggling to discipline our bodies and to refine our feelings. We see the pain of love in our eyes and the heat of conviction on our faces, and we realize that these things are good but that they are only touch points on a very long journey, and we receive the gift of spiritual insight.

For when we look at our lives in a spiritual way we come to understand why it is that we have been sent to the world by the Creator.

When in our symbolic journey to the West, we receive the gifts of prayer and meditation, we will come to know (though never completely), and then to love the Creator so intensely that the heat of that love will become a flame that devours all other love - much like the moth is devoured by the flame of the candle it is so unable to resist. And we will know that somehow this love fulfills one of the great purposes for which we have been created.

As we look from our watching place in the West and see ourselves struggling to learn the discipline of the South, we will realize that the journey to the four symbolic directions to receive the gifts and lessons of each of them fulfills another of the Creator's great purposes: that every human being should struggle (little by little, day by day) to develop herself to the fullest possible extent.

And then we will look over to the eastern horizons where our brother the eagle soars. We will see him there, ready to serve the people; ready to do all he can to help them make the journey of the medicine wheel together, so that their civilization might develop and flourish. Then we will realize that what he does we must all do in our own way. For such is the purpose of the Creator.

There are many other gifts the traveler may discover in the West, such as the gift of fasting, the gift of ceremony, the gift of clear self-knowledge, and the gift of vision. All are important, but the gift of vision is especially important.

The capacity to see clearly with our inner eye what we could become, or what the people could become together, if we should undertake the necessary journey, is as essential to human development as rain and sunshine are essential to the growth of plants. This is because as human beings we develop and grow through our own decisions. We therefore must have some vision, some ideal or goal to look toward, or else we will have no way of knowing what we must do. It is also vitally important that our vision be a true one. For many people believe themselves to be far less than what they could be. And because they cannot see any other possibility for themselves than their present undeveloped conditions, they stop struggling, and thereby abandon their (symbolic) journey around the medicine wheel.

In the youthfulness of the South the heart is drawn to goals and ideals, but these may, or may not be good goals or good ideals.

The inner spiritual vision learned from the symbolic teachers of the West aid us to judge our ideals, goals and actions against the spiritual understanding of what a human being really is, and of how beings progress.

D. The Gifts of the North

There is much the traveler can do to develop these gifts. The very first step is to realize that all may possess them. The way that they can be obtained, however, and even the way they will show themselves, will be slightly different for each person.

Much like the body of a great runner can be disciplined until it has learned tremendous endurance and great speed, so the mind can be trained until it becomes a highly developed instrument.

The North is the place of winter, of white snows that remind us of the white hair of our elders. It is the dawning place of true wisdom. Here dwell the teachers of intellectual gifts symbolized by the great mountain and the sacred lake. Some of the special gifts that await the traveler in the North of the medicine wheel include the following capacities:

    to think
    to synthesize
    to speculate
    to predict
    to discriminate
    to solve problems
    to imagine
    to analyze
    to understand
    to calculate
    to organize
    to criticize
    to remember
    to interpret hidden meanings

Like the warrior who begins training and is nearly overwhelmed by the sheer difficulty of running long distances or going without food for many days, travelers who wish to acquire the gifts of the North will often feel (at the beginning) that the task is too great or that they do not possess the necessary capacity to learn.

climb its slopes, the steeper and more difficult the way becomes. And yet the higher we go, the more we can see and the stronger we can become.

Let us take one gift, the gift of memory, and consider its development. We are not born with "poor memories". We are born with the capacity to learn and remember four and five languages at a time, and to be able to repeat exactly what we have seen and heard even if it is very complicated. One proof of this is that at the age of three or four years, you already knew nearly the entire language spoken in your community. Had you been born in China you would have spoken Chinese with the same ease that you now speak your own language. But over the years you have, for many reasons, stopped using that tremendous capacity to remember things that you were given by the Creator.

Yet one of the great lessons of the medicine wheel is that all human beings can acquire gifts in all of the symbolic directions. However, many of the gifts do not come automatically, or even easily. Often a decision is required, along with tremendous daily effort over a long period of time. The great mountain is one of the (symbolic) teachers of the North. The higher we

If you had not stopped, you would be able at will to repeat back the details of almost everything that you have ever heard, read, or thought in school or in your life. It is possible to learn how to do this. It is, through special training, possible to develop a memory so keen that you would be considered a genius wherever you went. It is possible, for example, to glance at 30 or 50 objects on a table or in a room, and then hours or even days later, to be able to repeat exactly the name and location of each object.

This and many other capacities of the mind are the birthright of every human being. We have only to journey (symbolically) to the North, and there to struggle. For nothing is gained without a price.

Completion

The North can also be seen as the direction of completion and fulfillment. Here the traveler learns the lessons of all things that end.

Here the powers of volition reach their zenith as we learn to complete what began as a far away vision. The capacity to finish what we have started is of tremendous importance to our well-being. This is the final lesson in the development of the powers of volition (the will).

We have learned from the teachers who dwell in the West, that the closer one gets towards the completion of a goal, the more difficult the journey becomes. To aid us in our life's struggles, the Creator has given the gift of perseverance. But even perseverance falters at the last without the certitude (sure knowledge) that the goal is near and can indeed be won.

Detachment

Access to the knowledge and wisdom required to judge whether or not the time of completion is indeed at hand is gained through the door of detachment. The gift of detachment bestows upon the traveler the ability to see the past, the present and the future as one.

Detachment means freedom from hate, jealousy, desire, anger and fear. It means a complete letting go of all things, even that which we love the best. It means being able to put behind us all the knowledge we have acquired on our journeys, for even knowledge itself can be a burden too heavy to carry to the summit of the great mountain and to the shores of the sacred lake.

To let go of something (like knowledge or love or hate) is not to throw it away. It is to step outside its shadow so that things may be seen in a different light.

It is difficult, but exceedingly important to learn how to stand apart from the things we believe to be true, or from our fears, our anger, our jealousy, our hate, or even from our love for someone. All of these can control us and prevent us from thinking clearly.

Fear, anger, jealousy, and hate can completely obscure a person's intelligence. Wise teachers say to avoid these as you would a poisonous snake. Love too can prevent a person from seeing clearly if it is not balanced by reason.

In order to acquire this art of standing apart from our strong feelings and thoughts, we must learn to look at ourselves from the center of the medicine wheel. From that center, we will be able to see how we fit together with everything else. We will experience ourselves to be a small but infinitely sacred part of a very large process.

When we dwell in that balanced center point, we cannot be controlled by our strong feelings or thoughts. From this sacred center, whatever action we take will be taken because we *decided* to act, and because it was good to do so.

When we can look at ourselves in this way, we will have learned the first lesson in detachment: that we are not our bodies, we are not our thoughts, we are not our feelings or our insights. We are something else far deeper and wider. We are the being that has thoughts, has insights. We are the being that feels and knows. We can watch our feelings, our thoughts, our insights and know them to be reflections in the mirror of the sacred lake.

The beginning of detachment is learned in the fires of love. The end of detachment is learned in quiet moments on the silent shores of the sacred lake, and cannot be told.

The Final Gift

It is possible for the traveler to be so enamoured with the gifts of any one of the directions that she may forget the journey and attempt to dwell forever with the teachers that have so captured her heart.

For example, a person may come to believe that having received the great intellectual gifts of the North, one has no need of further learning. There is great danger for the traveler, should she attempt to dwell forever in any of the directions. For the place of dwelling is in the center of the universe, and it is to the center that we must always return, for it is our true home.

Should a person abandon the journey because she feels she has found all that she needs in the gifts of one of the directions, great harm can come to her. For she

will have shut herself off from a large portion of her own true self, as well as created an imbalance that could seriously harm her.

A person who would dwell forever in the North, shutting out the gifts of the other directions, will become gripped with an icy coldness like that of winter, for she will be cut off from the warmth of her own heart.

Indeed, each of the gifts of each of the directions is balanced by other gifts. The boldness of the eagle is balanced by the humility of the willow and the prudence of the turtle. The idealism of the South is balanced by the wisdom and clarity of thought learned in the North.

The final lesson of the North is the lesson of balance, for wisdom teaches how all things fit together. And balance, when applied to the interconnectedness of all human beings, becomes justice. Justice is the greatest gift of the North. With its aid, the traveler can see all things as they really are. Without it, there can be no peace or security in the affairs of the world.

When we stand in the North, we can look over to the South and see ourselves singing the tender songs of love, and we realize that to know and understand is not only a thing of the head, but also of the heart. We can look to the East and there see the beautiful joy of our little mouse sister as she gazes at the western horizon, to the place of things unknown, and her marvelous ability to believe even though she cannot see. Then we realize that there is much more to be known than all the knowledge that all the wisest elders have ever known, and we are humbled.

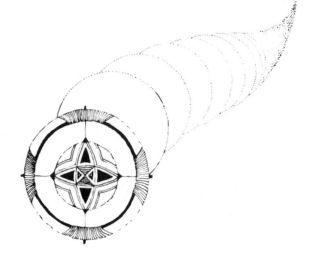

The mystery of all endings is found in the birth of new beginnings. There is no ending to the journey of the four directions. The human capacity to develop is infinite. The medicine wheel turns forever.

Summary Chart
The Gifts of the Four Directions

East

- light
- beginnings
- renewal
- innocence
- guilelessness
- spontaneity
- joy
- capacity to believe in the unseen
- warmth of spirit
- purity
- trust
- hope
- uncritical acceptance of others
- love that doesn't question others and doesn't know itself
- courage
- truthfulness
- birth
- rebirth
- childhood
- illumination
- guidance
- leadership

- beautiful speech
- vulnerability
- ability to see clearly through complex situations
- watching over others
- guiding others
- seeing situations in perspective
- hope for the people
- trust in your own vision
- ability to focus attention on present time tasks
- concentration
- devotion to the service of others

South

- youth
- fullness
- summer
- the heart
- generosity
- sensitivity to the feelings of others
- loyalty
- noble passions
- love (of one person for another)
- balanced development of the physical body
- physical discipline
- control of appetites
- determination
- goal setting
- training senses such as sight, hearing, taste
- musical development
- gracefulness
- appreciation of the arts
- discrimination in sight, hearing and taste
- passionate involvement in the world

- idealism
- emotional attraction to good and repulsion to bad
- compassion
- kindness
- anger at injustice
- repulsion by senseless violence
- feelings refined, developed, controlled
- ability to express hurt and other bad feelings
- ability to express joy and good feelings
- ability to set aside strong feelings in order to serve others

West

- darkness
- the unknown
- going within
- dreams
- deep inner thoughts
- testing of the will
- perseverance
- stick-to-it-iveness
- consolidating of personal power
- management of power
- spiritual insight
- daily prayer
- meditation
- fasting
- reflection
- contemplation
- silence
- being alone with one's self
- respect for elders
- respect for the spiritual struggles of others
- respect for others' beliefs

- awareness of our spiritual nature
- sacrifice
- humility
- love for the Creator
- commitment to the path of personal development
- commitment to universal life values and a high moral code
- commitment to struggle to assist the development of the people
- ceremony
- clear self-knowledge
- vision (a sense of possibilities and potentialities)

North

- elders
- wisdom
- thinking
- analyzing
- understanding
- speculating
- calculation
- prediction
- organizing
- categorizing
- discriminating
- criticizing
- problem solving
- imagining
- interpreting
- integrating all intellectual capacities
- completion
- fulfillment
- lessons of things that end
- capacity to finish what we begin
- detachment
- freedom from fear

- freedom from hate
- freedom from love
- freedom from knowledge
- seeing how all things fit together
- insight
- intuition made conscious
- sense of how to live a balanced life
- capacity to dwell in the center of things, to see and take the middle way
- moderation
- justice

VI. CODE OF ETHICS

In addition to the sacred teachings concerning the nature of things, and of the gifts of the four directions, the teachings of the *Sacred Tree* include a code of ethics to which all should conform their lives if they wish to find happiness and well-being. This code describes what wisdom means in the relationship between individuals, in family life, and in the life of the community. These are the sparkling gems of experience practiced by Native peoples everywhere. They represent the path of safety leading around the medicine wheel, and up the great mountain to the sacred lake. What follows is a summary of some of the most important of these teachings that are universal to all tribes.

1.

Each morning upon rising, and each evening before sleeping, give thanks for the life within you and for all life, for the good things the Creator has given you and others and for the opportunity to grow a little more each day. Consider your thoughts and actions of the past day and seek for the courage and strength to be a better person. Seek for the things that will benefit everyone.

2.

Respect. Respect means "to feel or show honor or esteem for someone or something; to consider the well-being of, or to treat someone or something with deference or courtesy". Showing respect is a basic law of life.

- Treat every person, from the tiniest child to the oldest elder with respect at all times.
- Special respect should be given to elders, parents, teachers and community leaders.
- No person should be made to feel "put down" by you; avoid hurting other hearts as you would avoid a deadly poison.
- Touch nothing that belongs to someone else (especially sacred objects) without permission, or an understanding between you.
- Respect the privacy of every person. Never intrude on a person's quiet moments or personal space.
- Never walk between people that are conversing.
- Never interrupt people who are conversing.
- Speak in a soft voice, especially when you are in the presence of elders, strangers or others to whom special respect is due.
- Do not speak unless invited to do so at gatherings where elders are present (except to ask what is expected of you, should you be in doubt).
- Never speak about others in a negative way, whether they are present or not.
- Treat the earth and all of her aspects as your mother. Show deep respect for the mineral world, the plant world, and the animal world. Do nothing to pollute the air or the soil. If others would destroy our mother, rise up with wisdom to defend her.
- Show deep respect for the beliefs and religions of others.
- Listen with courtesy to what others say, even if you feel that what they are saying is worthless. Listen with your heart.

3.

Respect the wisdom of the people in council. Once you give an idea to a council or a meeting it no longer belongs to you. It belongs to the people. Respect demands that you listen intently to the ideas of others in council and that you do not insist that your idea prevail. Indeed you should freely support the ideas of others if they are true and good, even if those ideas are quite different from the ones you have contributed. The clash of ideas brings forth the spark of truth.

Once a council has decided something in unity, respect demands that no one speak secretly against what has been decided. If the council has made an error, that error will become apparent to everyone in its own time.

4.

Be truthful at all times, and under all conditions.

5.

Always treat your guests with honor and consideration. Give of your best food, your best blankets, the best part of your house, and your best service to your guests.

6.

The hurt of one is the hurt of all, the honor of one is the honor of all.

7.

Receive strangers and outsiders with a loving heart and as members of the human family.

8.

All the races and tribes in the world are like the different coloured flowers of one meadow. All are beautiful. As children of the Creator they must all be respected.

9.

To serve others, to be of some use to family, community, nation or the world is one of the main purposes for which human beings have been created. Do not fill yourself with your own affairs and forget your most important task. True happiness comes only to those who dedicate their lives to the service of others.

10.

Observe moderation and balance in all things.

11.

Know those things that lead to your well-being, and those things that lead to your destruction.

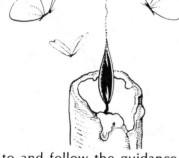

12.

Listen to and follow the guidance given to your heart. Expect guidance to come in many forms; in prayer, in dreams, in times of quiet solitude and in the words and deeds of wise elders and friends.

Conclusion

Gaining an understanding of the *Sacred Tree* is an eternal journey. As in all journeys, there must be time for activity, as well as rest.

It is our deep prayer that the Great Spirit will bless and guide your every step on this journey into an ever greater vision of beauty, truth, love, wisdom and justice, and that you will join us again in search of a greater understanding of the *Sacred Tree*.

To be continued . . .

Materials available from the Four World Development Project:

About the Project

Towards the Year 2000 — $6.00

Overview of the Four Worlds Development Project — $2.00

Resource Materials Being Used in Native Community Development

Taking Time to Listen: Using Community-based Research to Build Programs — $15.00

Developing Healthy Communities: Fundamental Strategies for Health Promotion — $12.00

Reaching for Wisdom: An Annotated Bibliography for the Prevention of Alcohol and Drug Abuse — $8.00

Integrated Community Development Planning — $5.00

The Four Worlds Exchange — Yearly Subscription $15.00 / Quarterly Journal of Resource Materials

Titles for Educators Working with Native Peoples

Wholistic Educational Evaluation — $6.00

Recreating Native Education: A Case Study in Program Evaluation and Design — $12.00

Handbook for Efffective School-Based Substance Abuse Prevention Program — $15.00

Culture: The Ultimate Curriculum — $6.00

Issues in Education Series — $2.50 each or $6.00 for three

The Four Worlds Community Education Series — $2.50 each or $20.50 for nine

Adult & Youth: The Shared Journey Toward Wholeness — $15.00

Educational Materials for Schools, Churches, Youth Groups and Service Organizations

The Sacred Tree Curriculum Package

This comprehensive package includes a curriculum guide, video, games, posters and other learning resources to complement the use of The Sacred Tree as a high school text. The program helps students assess their own lives in terms of the human potential for a balanced life guided by healthy values. $450.00

The Walking with Grandfather Curriculum Package

The six-part video and curriculum guide uses traditional North American Indian legends to help elementary school age children learn more about Native people while exploring basic human values such as caring for others, honesty, courage, and forgiveness. $320.00

The Unity in Diversity Curriculum Package

Designed for junior high students, this multicultural program includes a curriculum guide, posters, videos, games, and other learning resources. An in-depth case study of North American Indian issues is one of the many exciting activities in this experiential curriculum designed to promote tolerance and an appreciation for human diversity. $500.00

Catalog available with full description of each title as well as others — $1.00
Please add 10% shipping.

Enclose check or money order and mail to:

The Four Worlds Development Project
University of Lethbridge
4401 University Drive
Lethbridge, Alberta T1K 3M4
Tel (403) 328-4343 / Fax (403) 329-3081

BOOKS & TAPES FROM BLUE LOTUS
Audiotapes
Gifts to last and last! Native American tales for bedtime, alone time, or around the hearth.

HOPI
Reading & Storytelling from *Masked Gods, The Man Who Killed The Deer, The Book Of The Hopi*
by Frank Waters

Frank Waters has been associated with Native American storytelling since the early 1940s. His work in Southwestern mysticism, Pueblo life and Indian customs is admired as classic first-hand material. On this unusual cassette, Frank Waters tells stories and embroiders a spontaneous oral poetry based on his own writings, giving us a personal invitation to understand Native American tribal values with on of their most prominent interpreters. Music by Native American flutist, Robert Mirabal. (Boxed cassette — 5½''x8½'' — approx. 30 minutes.)

N. SCOTT MOMADAY
Storyteller

N. Scott Momaday, winner of Pulitzer Prize for the classic Native American novel, *House Made of Dawn*, tells stories of his Kiowa ancestry, a new legend of Billy the Kid, the great Fillmore Street Buffalo Drive in San Francisco, and a most unusual meeting with Georgia O'Keefe. Music is by Rust Crutcher. (Boxed audio cassette — 5½''x8½'' — approx. 1 hr.)

EYE OF CAT
The Story of Navajo Tracker
Billy Blackhorse Singer
by Roger Zelazny

Renowned science fiction fantasy author Roger Zelazny, winner of Hugo & Nebula Awards, reads his tale of a shape-shifting extraterrestrial chased by Navajo tracker, Billy Blackhorse Singer. A gripping confrontation of ancient mythology and fantastic future. Music by Ray Griffin. (Boxed set of 3 audio tapes — 5½''x8½'' — approx. 5 hours.)

NATIVE AMERICAN BOOKS & TAROT

SWIMMER THE SALMON
Native American Animal Stories
Narrated by Gerald Hausman / Music by Ray Griffin

In stories ranging from the Northeast to the Pacific Northwest, the legend of Turtle Island (North America) emerges. We hear of Killer Whale and Raven, Swimmer the Salmon and Turquoise Horse. These are the ways that brought Native Americans together with their animal counterparts. Collected from Hopi, Havajo, Iroquois, Kwakiutl, and Haida sources. Cassette $9.95

STARGAZER
A Native American Inquiry into Extraterrestrial Phenomena
by Gerald Hausman

A Navajo stargazer and medicine man, a French ufologist and an American poet join forces to probe one of the strangest mysteries in the Southwest. *Stargazer* is the true story of one man's emergence through Native American ritual into the world of psychic and extraterrestrial experience. From cattle mutilations to abductions in the deep realms of space, from peaceful Pueblos on the Rio Rande to jungle ruins in Cozumel, from formal interviews with tribal people to clandestine meetings, *Stargazer* focuses on myth, belief, and personal experience with the unexplainable. (219 pp.; 5½''x 8½''; also an audio cassette tape)

THE SACRED TREE

The Sacred Tree was created by the Four Worlds Development Project, a native American intertribal group, as a handbook of Native Spirituality for the indigenous peoples all over the Americas and the world. Through the guidanc of the tribal elders, Native values and traditions are being taught as the primary key to unlocking the force that will move Native peoples on the path of their own development. The elders have prophesied that by returning to traditional values, native societies can be transformed. This transformation would then have a healing effect on the entire planet.

The Sacred Tree is being used as handbook by the Four Worlds Development Project to eliminate widespread drug and alcohol abuse in tribal communities. It is now being shared for the first time with all members of the human family desiring personal growth.

THE SACRED TREE

THE FLIGHT OF FEATHERED SERPENT
The Xultun Tarot Deck
by Peter Balin

Peter Balin has lived among the Mopan Maya of Mexico. In *The Flight of Feathered Serpent,* he presents the authoritative guide to his Maya Tarot deck as well as an intimate look at one of the earliest advanced civilizations on Earth.

The Xultun Tarot Deck illuminates the traditional Tarot model in new and exciting ways: the cards are color-coded to the four Elements; the Lower Arcana are keyed to classical astrological symbols; and the Higher Arcana form a continuouis symbolic landscape. The deck is strong and lightweight and the 3½''x 5½'' cards are coated for endurance.

Blue Lotus Order Form

NATIVE AMERICAN TAPES, BOOKS AND TAROT

Ship To:

_____
Name of person receiving order

_____
Address

_____
Phone required if using P.O. Box
or Visa/Mastercard or personal check

☐ Charge to my   ☐ Visa ☐ Mastercard

_____
Authorized signature

_____
Card number   Exp. date month/year

☐ Check for total amount is enclosed.
I have figured all charges at right into my total amount. If shipping name is not the same as name on Visa/Mastercard, explain.

Total Order	$ _____
SHIPPING 10% or $3 minimum	$ _____
Wisconsin residents add 5% tax	$ _____
TOTAL ENCLOSED	$ _____

Cat. #	Quantity	AUDIO CASSETTES	Retail	Total
		HAUSMAN, GERALD		
990950		Navajo Nights	9.95	
990955		Stargazer	9.95	
990960		Swimmer the Salmon	9.95	
		STORYTELLER		
990975		N. Scott Momaday	12.95	
		WATERS, FRANK		
990965		Hopi	12.95	
		ZELAZNY, ROGER		
990980		Eye of Cat	24.95	

Cat. #	Quantity	BOOKS & TAROT	Retail	Total
990800		Flight of Feathered Serpent	13.95	
990805		Xultun (Mayan) Tarot Deck	13.95	
993090		Sacred Tree	9.95	
990925		Stargazer (Book I)	9.95	
990606		Sun Horse: Native Visions New World	14.95	

Request our catalog including Native American
Smudge Sticks & Supplies

Order from:
Blue Lotus
1-800-826-4810
Box 1008
Silver Lake, WI 53170
(Wholesale inquiries welcomed)
Note: Order Four Worlds Materials directly from Four Worlds. See page 84.